Witness History Series

THE ORIGINS OF WORLD WAR II

Peter Allen

The Bookwright Press
New York • 1992

Titles in this series

The Arab-Israeli Conflict
Blitzkrieg!
China since 1945
The Cold War
The Origins of World War I
The Origins of World War II
The Rise of Fascism
The Russian Revolution
South Africa since 1948
The Third Reich
The United Nations
The United States since 1945
The USSR under Stalin
War in the Trenches
War in Vietnam

Cover illustration: William Grupper's picture, portraying the Wall Street Crash of 1929. The worldwide depression that followed the Crash added to the instability of international relations in the 1930s.

First published in the
United States in 1992 by
The Bookwright Press
387 Park Avenue South
New York, NY 10016

First published in 1991 by
Wayland (Publishers) Limited
61 Western Road, Hove
East Sussex BN3 1JD, England

Library of Congress Cataloging-in-Publication Data
Allan, Peter.
    Origins of World War II/by Peter Allan.
       p. cm. – (Witness history)
    Includes bibliographical references and index.
    Summary: Explores the political and economic factors that
contributed to the outbreak of World War II. Includes quotations
from contemporary documents and sources.
    ISBN 0–531–18410–2
    1. World War, 1939–1945 – Causes – Juvenile literature. [1. World
War, 1939–1945 – Causes.] I. Title.   II Title. Origins of World
War Two.   III. Series: Witness history series.
D741.A47   1992
940.58'11 – dc20   91–22698
                                                        CIP
                                                        AC

Typeset by Kalligraphic Design Ltd, Horley, Surrey
Printed by G. Canale & C.S.p.A., Turin

Contents

1 **The aftermath of war**

The "peace" of Versailles   4
The League of Nations   6
The United States in isolation   8
"Never again"   10

2 **Dictatorships and depression**

Mussolini and Italy   12
The Soviet Union and Stalin   14
Japan emerges   16
China   18
The Depression   20

3 **Nazi Germany**

The Weimar Republic   22
Hitler's rise to power   24
The Nazis in power   26
Germany rearms   28

4 **Crisis and conflict in Europe**

The threat perceived?   30
Abyssinia and the Rhineland   32

The Spanish Civil War (1936–9)   34
Austria and Munich   36
War is declared   38

5 **The East**

Japanese militarism   40
Japan and China at war   42
Japan and the Soviet Union   44

6 **From war to world war**

The end of U.S. isolationism   46
Barbarossa   48
Pearl Harbor   50

Leading figures   52

Important dates   56

Glossary   58

Further reading   60

Notes on sources   61

Index   62

1
THE AFTERMATH OF WAR
The "peace" of Versailles

ON NOVEMBER 11, 1918, an armistice – or ceasefire – ended World War I. The war had lasted for four years and had been fought by the powers of the Triple Entente (Britain, Russia and France) together with their allies, including the United States, against Germany and Austria-Hungary. The President of the United States, Woodrow Wilson, declared the war had been fought to make the world safe for democracy and for small nations. Yet only twenty years later another great war was about to begin. Why did the peace not last, and what caused this second world war, which resulted in even greater death and devastation than the first?

In January 1919, representatives of the warring nations met at the Paris Peace Conference to agree to the terms upon which peace could be secured. The United States was represented by its president, Woodrow Wilson. In January 1918 he had laid down "fourteen points" according to which he wanted the peace to be arranged: these included the re-

placement of secret diplomacy with open negotiation between nations; arms reduction; freedom to trade; and the creation of new nation states according to the principle of "self-determination." According to this principle, the people of every nationality would be able to choose the conditions in which they lived.

France was represented by Georges Clemenceau, the prime minister. He wanted to disarm Germany and create a number of independent states in Eastern Europe out of the ruins of the Austro-Hungarian Empire. He would thereby protect French interests and ensure his country's security. Clemenceau also wanted to make Germany pay reparations – fines paid by the losing side in a war to make up for the damage caused.

Britain's prime minister, David Lloyd George, wanted to make the British Empire safe by confiscating German colonies and reducing the German naval fleet so that Germany would never be a threat to Britain's security again.

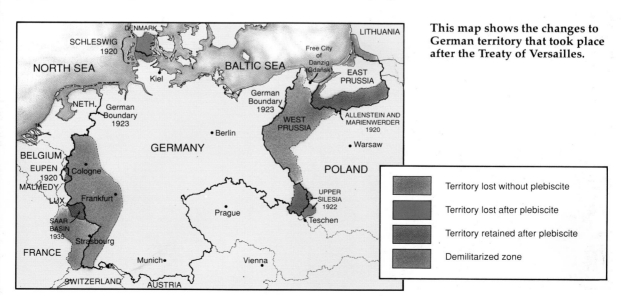

This map shows the changes to German territory that took place after the Treaty of Versailles.

Legend:
- Territory lost without plebiscite
- Territory lost after plebiscite
- Territory retained after plebiscite
- Demilitarized zone

Germany had surrendered believing that Wilson's "fourteen points" would be the basis of a negotiated peace. In fact, the victorious powers' terms were not negotiable and the German delegation was advised to take them or leave them. Under these terms, which became the Treaty of Versailles, Germany lost territory, in particular Alsace-Lorraine, consisting of two large provinces on the French-German border. Germany was forbidden to unite with Austria, and its colonies were confiscated. It was to pay reparations, although the amount was not yet decided. It lost its air force, tanks and submarines, and it was to have only a small army and navy. Finally, the Germans were even expected to admit that the war had been their fault.

In Germany, the treaty was unpopular. The loss of German territory in Europe and the ban on union with Austria were contrary to Wilson's principle of self-determination. Many Germans thought that their country would be unable to pay reparations and would collapse economically. Others thought it was unfair to impose the conditions for peace without negotiations.

Even some people outside Germany thought the treaty was unfair. John Maynard Keynes, a British economist who attended the Conference at Versailles, questioned the morality and the wisdom

> . . . of reducing Germany to servitude for a generation, of degrading the lives of millions of human beings, and of depriving a whole nation of happiness . . . [1]

He was convinced that the harsh treaty was short-sighted.

▲ A German cartoon shows the Devil with his cronies Greed (*Habgier*), Revenge (*Rachsucht*) and Lust for Power (*Machtkitzel*) gloating at the Treaty of Versailles.

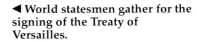

◀ World statesmen gather for the signing of the Treaty of Versailles.

The League of Nations

A cartoon from *Punch*, the British satirical magazine.

MORAL SUASION.

THE RABBIT. "MY OFFENSIVE EQUIPMENT BEING PRACTICALLY *NIL*, IT REMAINS FOR ME TO FASCINATE HIM WITH THE POWER OF MY EYE."

One of the principles advanced by President Wilson at the Paris Peace Conference was the creation of a "League of Nations."

Many people believed that World War I had been made inevitable by the international arms race that preceded it. The new League of Nations was intended to provide "collective security." Instead of having to enter into dangerous alliances or manufacture armaments in order to survive, nations could look to the other countries in the League to provide support – even armed forces – to defend them against aggression.

The League of Nations played a large part in creating the atmosphere of international peace that characterized the 1920s. As an official of the League of Nations later put it, the founders of the League wanted to prevent the re-creation of

. . . the elaborate system of alliances that dragged nation after nation into the War, as soon as the spark was ignited in some remote spot. [2]

The League's structure was set out in a document called the "Covenant." All member nations met in an Assembly once a year. The League also had a Council, formed by representatives of the major powers, plus a number of smaller countries elected by the Assembly. There was a Secretariat to administer the League. All members had to register international treaties publicly, so there could be no secret agreements. They also had to provide full information about their military spending, and any international dispute was to be settled by negotiation. Article 16 of the Covenant stated:

A mutual undertaking is given by the Members of the League to combine (by diplomatic pressure, blockade or if necessary armed force) to prevent a resort to war in breach of . . . the Covenant. [3]

However, the League did not succeed in achieving its aims. The League's biggest weakness was that the largest and most powerful countries of the world were never fully committed to it. Although the idea behind the League had come from an American, Woodrow Wilson, the United States itself never joined. Germany was not allowed to join until 1926, and Russia not until 1934. In any case, the German government, backed by public support, decided to leave the League in 1933. Japan left in the same year. In the 1930s, even Britain and France began to rearm and make alliances – some secret – to provide their security. The League was eventually to become more and more irrelevant.

The Tenth Annual Assembly of the League of Nations in Geneva in 1929. The speaker is Aristide Briand, the French prime minister. Despite being beset with problems, the League did at first help to create an atmosphere of international peace in the 1920s.

The United States in isolation

The United States came out of World War I much stronger economically then when it had entered the war. Its political influence on the international stage was stronger too. It had helped prevent a German victory in the war, and with President Wilson insisting on a moral and just peace, many people believed the United States should play an active role in the peacemaking process. However, after the Paris Peace Conference, the nation rapidly withdrew from world affairs, adopting a policy called "isolationism."

Isolationism was not new to the United States. In 1796, George Washington, the first president, said:

> *It is our true policy to steer clear of permanent alliances with any portion of the foreign world.*[4]

In 1919, there were still many Americans who agreed with Washington's words, and when Wilson returned from Paris he found that the Treaty of Versailles was unpopular. Some people felt it was unfair to Germany; some disapproved of Britain and France having empires, and believed that the League of Nations would act as a sort of "super-state," run by Britain and France, which would limit American freedom of action. Some members of the Senate were annoyed that Wilson had not taken any Senators with him to Paris. As a result, the Senate refused to approve the Treaty of Versailles or to allow the United States to join the League.

American isolationism showed itself in other ways. The United States attempted to

There was much dismay in Europe at the failure of the United States to ratify the Treaty of Versailles and join the League of Nations.

THE GAP IN THE BRIDGE.

◄ Calvin Coolidge, U.S. president 1925–9, portrayed in 1928 as the creator of American prosperity and peace. A year later the prosperity looked less secure.

▼ Warren Harding – U.S. president 1921–3. He called for a "return to normalcy" after World War I and opposed the League of Nations.

protect its industry from foreign competition by imposing high import duties. The U.S. government was also asked by the other Allies to treat the money it had loaned to them during World War I as America's contribution to winning the war. President Warren G. Harding, who replaced Wilson in 1921, refused to view the "war debts" in this light and insisted that all these foreign debts be paid. Calvin Coolidge, who became president in 1924, is reputed to have said:

> *They hired the money, didn't they?* [5]

In fact, the United States eventually accepted that it should recover only a proportion of its war debts, as this table[6] shows:

Country	Amount due ($m)	Percentage of debt canceled
Belgium	418	53.5
Britain	4,600	19.7
France	4,025	52.8
Italy	2,042	75.4

The United States also limited its isolationism in other ways. It held a conference at Washington in 1921–2 to discuss Asian and Pacific affairs with eight other countries, including Britain, France and Japan; and in 1928 the American secretary of state, Frank B. Kellogg, and the French foreign minister, Aristide Briand, sponsored a pact outlawing all war, signed by all the world's governments.

"Never again"

World War I made a deep impression on the two great European democracies, Britain and France. It left them both groping for guarantees of peace, but in different ways.

In Britain, the horrors of trench warfare had largely been kept secret from the public. When the troops returned in 1918 and 1919, people were appalled by what they learned. The public mood in Britain became deeply pacifist. The king, George V, speaking to Lloyd George, said:

> I will **not** have another war. I **will not**. [7]

This pacifism was reflected in British foreign policy. With Germany weakened and largely disarmed by the Treaty of Versailles and with the Soviet Union also weak, the British government felt it was safe to save money and gain popularity by vastly reducing spending on armaments. Winston Churchill was chancellor of the exchequer in 1924, and he reduced defense expenditure greatly. After 1919, British defense spending was calculated according to the "ten year rule" – the assumption that Britain would not need to take part in any major war for ten years. This rule was not abolished until 1932, when war was, in fact, only seven years away.

The French attitude was slightly different. Although pacifism was an even stronger force in French politics, the fear of a revived Germany also remained a major influence on French foreign policy. This was why Clemenceau had been so eager to protect French interests at the Paris Peace Conference.

Winston Churchill in 1919 when he was the British government minister responsible for the army. In 1924 he became chancellor of the exchequer and reduced spending on defense.

▲ **French troops occupying Germany's industrial heartland, the Ruhr. They were met with passive resistance.**

The French wanted to see the Treaty of Versailles followed rigorously. They pressed hard for a very high level of reparations payments. In 1923, when Germany failed to pay on time, French and Belgian troops occupied the Ruhr – Germany's chief coal-mining and industrial region. Some members of the French government wanted to create a small independent state in the Rhineland. Furthermore, France constructed a network of alliances with the newly created states in Eastern Europe, to encircle Germany.

The different approaches of Britain and France were summed up by a British official:

> *The fact is that [the French] wanted a stronger treaty and we wanted an easier one . . . from the first we always intended to ease up the execution of the treaty if the Germans played the game.* [8]

If the Germans "behaved themselves," the British were prepared to be lenient.

J'Y SUIS—J'Y RESTE.

France ("RF" stands for "Republic of France") saying, "Here I am – here I stay."

2

DICTATORSHIPS AND DEPRESSION
Mussolini and Italy

LIKE MOST EUROPEAN COUNTRIES, Italy emerged from World War I weakened by high inflation, low economic output and political instability. It had lost well over half a million men but gained very little of the territory it had originally been promised by the other Allies. Strikes and a fear of revolution now caused many well-off people to hope for strong government.

Benito Mussolini was originally a militant left-wing journalist who had fought for the Italian army during World War I. He was politically ambitious, and after the war he formed a party to profit from the fear of rev-

olution and strikes. He collected violent young men as *squadristi* – semi-military mobs who would attack left-wing activists. Mussolini quickly became popular with conservatives, and when, in October 1922, he used his *squadristi* to threaten the government with armed revolution, King Victor Emmanuel chose to submit to his threats rather than use the army against them. Mussolini was appointed prime minister.

A fascist propaganda painting showing the supposed change from communist-inspired destruction and civil war (*Bolscevismo*) to peace and prosperity under Mussolini (*Fascismo*).

1919 -Bolscevismo-　　　*1923 -Fascismo-*

Mussolini called his political program "fascism." It was opposed to democracy. Opposition politicians were removed from government and sometimes murdered. The Chamber of Deputies – parliament – became much less important and was eventually abolished. Fascism relied greatly on propaganda that sought to portray Mussolini as a heroic, violent, energetic revolutionary. Giovanni Gentile, an important propagandist for the regime, wrote:

> *The Italian people have set out with a faith and a passion . . . They are on the march, obedient and disciplined as never before . . . with their eyes fixed on the man of heroic mold . . . He strides ahead, the instrument elected by Providence to create a new civilization.*[9]

Fascist economic policy aimed to reduce trade union strength and increase the government's control of industry. An important

With his hands on hips, Mussolini poses with Italian army veterans and fascist *squadristi*.

component of fascism was the cult of war. Mussolini wrote:

> *War alone brings up to their highest tension all human energies and puts the stamp of nobility upon the peoples who have the courage to meet it. All other trials are substitutes . . .*[10]

With this brand of fascism, Mussolini promoted an aggressive and warlike foreign policy. He wanted to increase Italy's prestige abroad and dreamed of an Italian colonial empire stretching across central Africa. More immediately, he wanted to oppose Greek influence in the Adriatic Sea. In 1923 his troops occupied the Greek island of Corfu, but Mussolini bowed to world public opinion and withdrew them after a month. Throughout the 1920s, he attempted to increase Italy's influence in Albania. However, in the 1920s, Mussolini was not recognized as a threat by Britain and France. He was regarded as a "bulwark [defense] against Bolshevism," and diplomatic relations between the countries remained good.

The Soviet Union and Stalin

In October 1917 the government of Russia was overthrown by a communist revolution. The Russian communists, or Bolsheviks, stood for a radical, left-wing program; their leader, Vladimir Ilyich Lenin, wanted

> . . . to place power in the hands of the proletariat and the poorest strata of the peasantry. [11]

The banks and all land were to be controlled by the state, and the police and army were to be abolished. In the unstable economic climate after World War I, this program was viewed with great suspicion by other governments, who feared that revolution might spread to Europe.

Some Western governments sent troops to Russia to help stop the revolution from

▲ Lenin addresses Soviet troops in Moscow's Red Square, 1919. Lenin led the Bolsheviks in the October Revolution of 1917, which established the Soviet government.

spreading from Moscow and Petrograd to the countryside. They were unsuccessful. However, this interference made the Bolsheviks very distrustful of the Western countries.

The mutual suspicion was made worse by the Bolsheviks' declared aim of spreading revolution wherever they could. They set up the Communist International, or Comintern, in 1919, to encourage uprisings and economic collapse among Western countries. This unrest, they believed, would lead to international revolution. In addition, the Bolsheviks refused to pay the debts incurred by the previous government of Russia. They irritated the United States, and the U.S. government did not formally recognize the Bolshevik gov-

◀ Leon Trotsky photographed in 1920 when he was Soviet commissar for war. After Lenin's death, Trotsky lost the political battle for the leadership of the Communist Party and was deported from the Soviet Union in 1929. He was assassinated by Stalin's agents in 1940 while living as an exile in Mexico.

▼ A Soviet poster from 1930 proclaiming the modernization of the coal-mining industry. The text reads: "We shall mechanize the coalfield."

ernment in Russia – now called the Union of Soviet Socialist Republics (USSR) – until 1933.

In 1924 Lenin died, and there was a political battle for the leadership of the Communist Party between Leon Trotsky and Josef Stalin. Stalin wanted to concentrate on reforming industry and agriculture within the Soviet Union, without involving the new state in foreign affairs. His policy was called "socialism in one country." Trotsky disagreed with this form of Soviet isolationism. He believed that communism in the Soviet Union would never be safe until the whole world was Bolshevik.

Nikolai I. Bukharin, a senior Bolshevik, described the dispute in this way:

> The controversy is over this: can we build socialism and complete the building if we leave aside international affairs?[12]

Trotsky replied sarcastically:

> You can go for a walk naked in the streets of Moscow in the month of January – if you leave aside the weather.[12]

Stalin finally gained control of the Communist Party, and as a result, after 1926 the Soviet Union withdrew from the international scene. At home, Stalin consolidated his position and became a dictator. He ruthlessly pursued a policy to reorganize agriculture and develop industry. One of his main aims was to prevent the Soviet Union from being involved in a major war, which would put this program of reorganization and development in danger.

Japan emerges

At the end of the nineteenth century, a new world power emerged in the Far East – Japan. From being a backward, isolated country, Japan rapidly developed modern industry and adopted a European-style legal system and parliament. The Japanese also built up powerful armed forces.

As it modernized, Japan soon showed a strong desire to expand onto the East Asian mainland. Its foreign policy was governed by a fear of Russia, the only other country in the region that was powerful enough to challenge its ambitions. In 1902, Japan signed an alliance with Britain to give it some protection against Russia.

In 1904 Japan fought and won a war against Russia. This was the first time an Asian country had defeated a great European power; so by 1914, Japan was already accepted as a full-fledged member of the international community. Japan's importance was made clear after the war, when it was given a permanent seat on the Council of the League of Nations.

During the 1920s and 1930s, many Japanese people debated their country's foreign policy. They discussed two broad issues. First, some people thought that Western influence was far too strong. Should Japan oppose the colonial influence of Britain, France, the Netherlands and the United States in the Far East? One extreme nationalist, who had murdered a Japanese businessman with Western connections, said:

> *This is a time of danger . . . foreign thought . . . has moved in like a rushing torrent.* [13]

The second question was how Japan's power in the region could be increased. Some Japanese, particularly those in the army,

◀ Japanese troops on the march during the 1904 Russo-Japanese war. Japan won the war – the first time an Asian country had defeated a European power.

▶ A Japanese print celebrating the occupation of Port Arthur in Manchuria during the war with Russia in 1904.

thought that Japan should invade areas of the East Asian mainland, though there was disagreement about where was best: Manchuria or China.

During the 1920s, however, the Japanese government pursued a cautious foreign policy. In 1922, at the Washington Naval Conference, Britain, France, Japan and the United States agreed to consult in the event of any future crisis. Limits were set on the number of battleships in the Pacific Ocean and how large and powerful their guns were to be. Most important, nine countries, including Japan, agreed not to intervene in Chinese affairs. These agreements replaced the 1902 Anglo-Japanese Alliance.

In Japan, many people still discussed how the country might expand. Yet, in the 1920s, Japan's acceptance of what became known as the "Washington Conference System" showed that it seemed willing to conform to Western ideas about "collective security."

China

Chiang Kai-shek (right) and Feng Yu-hsiang, a powerful warlord in northern China who joined forces with the KMT in 1928.

While Japan was modernizing rapidly, China, the other great power in the Far East, seemed to be in decline. It had five times the population of Japan but had little modern industry and was permanently close to civil war. In the 1920s, the whole of East Asia was made unstable by this dangerous combination of a weak, vulnerable China and a powerful, potentially aggressive Japan.

The Ch'ing dynasty in China, which had ruled since the seventeenth century, was finally overthrown after revolution erupted in 1911. Central government virtually collapsed, and throughout most of China political power passed into the hands of local military leaders who were called "warlords." In some parts of the Chinese empire, outsiders took control: Mongolia came under Russian influence; Tibet and western China became more or less independent; and Manchuria was occupied by Japan. As a result of treaties dating mostly from the nineteenth century, a number of ports on the Chinese coast were effectively Western colonies.

The Kuomintang (Chinese Nationalist Party or KMT) was formed in 1912–13, and during the 1920s power in China was increasingly in its hands. This political party stood for Chinese nationalism, the introduction of Western ideas and moderate socialism. Its army gradually took over more and more of China. The Chinese Communist Party allied itself with the KMT. The Soviet Union, eager at this stage to spread revolution, financed and advised the KMT's army.

In 1926, one of the KMT's generals, Chiang Kai-shek, took over the KMT. He realized that Stalin was only using the KMT as a device to foster communist revolution. Indeed, Stalin had said of the KMT:

> They have to be utilized to the end, squeezed like a lemon, then thrown away. [14]

A KMT cartoon depicting Chiang Kai-shek (in the circle) and Nationalist successes against the communists. Under Chiang's leadership, the KMT tried to resist Japanese aggression.

In Shanghai in April 1927, Chiang Kai-Shek had the local communists massacred, and Stalin's bid for power in China was ended.

As Chiang's power increased throughout China, he became a dictator. Yet he remained on good terms with Western countries, particularly the United States. He was a strongly nationalist leader who always tried to resist Japanese aggression. During 1927 and 1928, Nationalist Chinese troops and the Japanese army in Manchuria clashed on a number of occasions. At the end of 1928, the local ruler of Manchuria, Chang Hseuh-liang, stopped supporting Japanese ambitions there and switched sides to support Chiang Kai-shek's Chinese Nationalist Party.

The Depression

By about 1925 Europe and the United States had recovered economically from the effects of World War I. From then until 1929 most industrial countries experienced an economic boom. Industrial production, international trade and investment of savings all increased at a faster rate than the rise in prices. Germany was now able to pay reparations regularly, and a program of repayments, called the Dawes Plan, was agreed upon in 1924. In 1925 the British government decided to link the value of the pound sterling to the internationally agreed price of gold – the so-called gold standard. This return to pre-1914 practices increased confidence in the health of the British economy. The other major European currencies – the French franc and the German Reichsmark – were similarly stabilized. Investment in stock markets – where companies can raise capital by issuing shares – increased sharply, especially in the United States. Prices of shares on the New York Stock Exchange reached record levels.

In 1929 this mood of confidence was destroyed. In the summer there were signs that the economic boom was over. Building and car production slowed down in the United States and unemployment increased in Germany. The harvest was very good in the United States and Canada; too much food was produced, and prices fell sharply. On October 24, 1929, the New York Stock Exchange reacted to these signs, and share prices fell dramatically. This was called the "Wall Street Crash." American businessmen lost any hope that the boom would continue.

Investment in industry fell sharply, and many consumers had less money to spend because they had lost their savings in the Crash. More and more people in the United States were forced out of work. To try to raise cash, American firms and investors asked for the return of money they had loaned to companies abroad – thus affecting Europe too. There the prices of both food and industrial goods fell. Farmers produced more to maintain their incomes, which forced prices down further. Eventually, people became so worried that they withdrew their money from many banks, which could no longer advance to firms the money they needed to pay for raw materials or wages.

This cycle of reducing production, reducing prices, a weakened banking system and

A demonstration against unemployment in the United States.

increasing unemployment was called the "Great Depression." It affected all countries, although not at exactly the same time or in the same way.

Did the Depression help to cause World War II? Certainly the effects in Germany contributed to the rise to power of Adolf Hitler. In Japan, worldwide depression had reduced foreign demand for Japanese exports, particularly silk, and the price of rice fell. This caused particular distress in the Japanese countryside, where peasant farmers supported the army's plans for expansion and conquest. In Britain and France, the Depression made the governments less willing to spend money on arms to deter an aggressive Germany.

The reduction in international trade may have led to a mood of international hostility in the 1930s. However, the world economy was recovering by the mid-1930s, and the Depression does not seem to have greatly influenced events in the three or four years immediately before the outbreak of war.

▲ A British cartoon entitled "The Patient Gentlemen of England" depicts unemployed working men in Britain against a background of newspaper reports of violence elsewhere in Europe.

◀ A poster, "Industrial Giant," proclaiming the success of Roosevelt's New Deal program of government spending, which created new jobs and rescued the U.S. economy from the effects of the Depression.

3
NAZI GERMANY
The Weimar Republic

WHEN THE OLD IMPERIAL GOVERNMENT of Germany collapsed in 1918, its place was taken by the democratic Weimar Republic.

The first years of the Weimar Republic were marked by political and economic instability. There were communist uprisings in Berlin and southern Germany, and for a time it looked as though the Republic would not survive at all. Most Germans thought the Treaty of Versailles was very unfair and should be changed. The economy had been weakened by the war, and in 1923, the government could no longer pay reparations. As a result, French and Belgian troops occupied the Ruhr industrial region. They used violence to put down a strike by the workers there.

The occupation of the Ruhr in 1923 only worsened the economic crisis. People lost confidence in the German currency, and inflation rose, at first slowly and then faster and faster. The value of money fell so much that people had to use thousands, and then millions of banknotes to pay for the simplest

A political poster promising a brighter future for Germany after the 1924 Reichstag elections. Between 1924 and 1929 the Weimar Republic enjoyed a brief period of political and economic stability.

things. Savings lost their value virtually overnight. A contemporary song went:

> We are drinking away our Grandma's little
>   capital
> And her first and second mortgages too. [15]

The working class were especially hard hit by this inflation.

One man who tried to exploit the popular discontent was Adolf Hitler, leader of the extreme right-wing *Nationalsozialistische Deutsche Arbeiterpartei* (the National Socialist German Workers', or Nazi, Party). The Nazis' answer to Germany's problems was a combination of extreme German nationalism, which defied the Treaty of Versailles, and opposition to capitalism. In 1923, Hitler declared a revolution, or *Putsch*, in Munich. However, the uprising collapsed when conservatives and

the army failed to support it. The chief of the army staff, General Hans von Seeckt, said:

> Ha, comic happenings in Munich this evening …
> There is revolution. [16]

Hitler was arrested and sentenced to five years' imprisonment. In fact, his sentence was soon reduced to thirteen months.

In the mid-1920s, the German economy began to revive. Under the American Dawes Plan, which was accepted in 1924, Germany's annual reparation payments were reduced, and Germany received more loans from the United States. Gustav Stresemann, the German foreign minister, also improved Germany's image abroad. He signed the Treaty of Locarno in 1925, which formally accepted the Treaty of Versailles, and Germany was admitted to the League of Nations.

Yet Germany remained isolated and fearful of French aggression. Secretly, Stresemann arranged for the small German army to conduct weapons training in the Soviet Union.

Gustav Stresemann with other international statesmen at the Conference of Locarno in 1925. Mussolini, Beneš and Briand were among those attending.

Hitler's rise to power

LISTE: 9

NATIONAL-SOZIALISTISCHE
DEUTSCHE-
ARBEITER-PARTEI

◀ A Nazi poster of 1930 promises death to, among other things, Versailles, Locarno, Bolshevism, inflation and the Jews. In the 1930s, support for the Nazi Party rose dramatically thanks to an effective propaganda campaign that exploited many of the fears and grievances that were widespread among Germans at the time.

When Hitler was released from prison in 1924, the German economy had begun to recover and Hitler's support had somewhat fallen away. He spent the next few years rebuilding the Nazi Party and absorbing the other extreme right-wing groups. Then, the Wall Street Crash of October 1929 had a devastating effect on the Weimar Republic. Unemployment rose rapidly:

Year	No. of unemployed in millions[17]
July 1928	1.012
Jan. 1930	3.218
Jan. 1931	4.887
Jan. 1932	6.042
Jan. 1933	6.014

By the winter of 1931–2, about one in every two families was affected by unemployment. As farm prices fell, hardship in agricultural areas worsened.

In this crisis, the Nazi Party found a popular response to its anti-Weimar propaganda. Nazi propaganda exploited the unhappiness caused by unemployment, grievances about Versailles and the memories of inflation. It was particularly effective in the rural areas of north Germany, where the moderate political parties associated with the Roman Catholic Church were weakest. Hundreds of thousands of unemployed youths joined the *Sturmabteilung* or *SA* (the Nazi terrorist militia) and the *Schutzstaffel* or *SS* (Hitler's "protection squad"), which went around beating up opponents, notably the communists.

Electoral support for the Nazi Party rose spectacularly – the election results of 1930 showed how effective the Nazi strategy was. It had 18 percent of the vote and became the second largest party in the Reichstag, the German parliament.

Division among the other political parties played into Hitler's hands. No single party had a majority in parliament, and the coalition government was split. The main right-wing party, the German National Party, refused to support the moderate Catholic government of Heinrich Brüning. Because Brüning could no longer command a majority in the Reichstag, he had to rule by decree. However, his policies failed to halt the Depression, and in a presidential election in April 1932, Hitler's share of the vote rose to one-third, making the Nazis easily the largest single party.

The Nazis and communists were now fighting in the streets with increasing violence. In this atmosphere, Brüning opened talks with Hitler to see whether he could get his support. Once firmly in power, Brüning believed he would be able to manipulate

Hitler. But Brüning failed to win Hitler over and had to resign in May 1932.

Franz von Papen was now made chancellor, and he too courted Hitler's support. However, Hitler demanded to be chancellor himself. The situation was becoming desperate, and many people feared that political instability would lead to a communist revolution. Von Papen again approached Hitler, and on January 30 Hitler was appointed chancellor. Von Papen, now Hitler's deputy, said to a colleague:

> *Within two months we will have pushed Hitler so far into a corner that he'll squeak.* [18]

Von Papen was fatally deluded in believing that he could manipulate Hitler.

Adolf Hitler with a group of young National Socialists in 1923.

The Nazis in power

When Hitler was appointed chancellor he did not have absolute power. Like Brüning, he could rule by decree, but he needed the support of the president, the veteran soldier Field Marshal Von Hindenburg. There were only three Nazis in the cabinet.

Then, on February 27, 1933, the Reichstag building was gutted by fire. Hitler immediately blamed the communists, and he used the fire as an excuse to ban the Communist Party and declare martial law. New elections were then called, and in an atmosphere of fear and panic, the Nazis won 43.9 percent of the votes cast.

Although he still did not have an absolute majority, Hitler now asked the Reichstag to pass an Enabling Act, which would give him emergency powers to rule without the approval of parliament or the president. He employed all his resources of propaganda to convince the Catholic and other right-wing parties to agree, emphasizing the communist threat and playing on their nationalist sympathies. For the critical vote in the Reichstag,

Adolf Hitler, recently made chancellor, greets President Hindenburg of Germany.

even stronger tactics were used. One of the socialist deputies who wanted to vote against Hitler wrote:

> We were received with wild choruses: "We want the Enabling Act." Youths with swastikas on their chests eyed us insolently, blocked our way . . . When we . . . had taken our seats, SA and SS men lined up . . . behind us in a semi-circle.[19]

The Enabling Act was passed, and during the summer of 1933 Hitler banned all political parties other than the Nazis.

Hitler was also quick to extinguish any opposition within the Nazi movement. The notorious *SA* was becoming difficult to control, and its head, Ernst Röhm, clashed with the professional German army officers whose support Hitler now needed. Early on June 30, 1934, Hitler had most of the senior officers of the *SA* shot. From then on he could operate without opposition.

Hitler and his Nazi leadership built a vast apparatus of terror and repression in Germany. The membership of the *SS* grew from 50,000 to 250,000 between 1934 and 1939. The Gestapo, or state secret police, arrested and murdered people whom they wanted to suppress. Communists, socialists, gypsies and homosexuals were forced into concentration camps. Much Nazi persecution was directed at the Jews. During the 1930s, about 300,000

Jews emigrated. The horrors of the holocaust awaited those who stayed.

Hitler's position grew stronger. The worst of the Depression was over before Hitler became chancellor, but Nazi policies also had a positive effect on Germany's economy. Between 1933 and 1936 the Nazis organized work-creation programs and invested in the car industry and large public construction projects, such as superhighways. Unemployment fell. After 1936, rearmament became more and more important.

▲ The Reichstag burns. Many people believed the Nazis started the fire.

◄ Germans give the Nazi salute over a pile of condemned books they are burning.

27

Germany rearms

As Hitler consolidated his power within Germany, other European governments became anxious about the kind of foreign policy that the new fascist regime would adopt. Historians debate to what extent Hitler had a coherent plan to seize power and to expand Germany's territory eastward, and to what extent his actions were the result of opportunism and exploitation of events.

In 1924, while in prison following the Munich *Putsch*, Hitler had written about his political ideas. His book, *Mein Kampf* (*My Struggle*), contained long passages expressing Hitler's hatred of the Jews, references to the weakness of democracy, criticisms of the Treaty of Versailles and a hazy plan for German expansion eastward. In 1948, Winston Churchill wrote:

> *There was no book which deserved more careful study from the rulers, both political and military, of the Allied powers. All was there . . .*[20]

Some German policemen demonstrate their allegiance to Hitler at a sports festival in Berlin.

In fact, some historians have questioned how far *Mein Kampf* could have really been used to predict Hitler's intentions. For example, Hitler wrote:

> *For a long time yet to come there will be only two powers in Europe with which it may be possible for Germany to conclude an alliance. These powers are Great Britain and Italy.*[21]

This was hardly an accurate prediction concerning Germany's future allies.

Even though *Mein Kampf* did not lay out Hitler's foreign policy plans exactly, it soon became clear that the Nazis had a very different policy from that of Stresemann during the Weimar Republic. During Hitler's first year as chancellor, Germany withdrew from the League of Nations. In an interview with a British newspaper, the *Daily Mail*, Hitler said:

> *The League has no future . . . it is intolerable for us that we should continually and repeatedly be dishonored and humiliated.*[22]

The Nazi Party rally at Nuremberg in 1934. The helmets in the foreground belong to members of the SS.

The harsh Treaty of Versailles still rankled with most Germans, and Hitler's attitude gained him further support within Germany.

In February 1933, contrary to the Treaty of Versailles, Germany began to rearm in secret. In January 1934, Hitler started to make old-fashioned alliances, rather than using the collective security of the League. He signed a nonaggression pact with Poland. By March 1935 men were being openly conscripted into the armed forces, and by 1938 Germany had some of the strongest armed forces in Europe.

How were other European countries to react to German rearmament? Britain, France and Italy met at the Italian resort of Stresa and agreed to oppose German expansion. However, Britain also came to a separate agreement with Germany, whereby Britain allowed the German navy to expand, as long as it remained smaller than a third of the size of the British navy. As the 1930s wore on, there was to be great debate, particularly in Britain and France, about how to respond to the new German threat.

A cartoon of 1936 portrays the new Germany burying the ghost of Versailles.

4
CRISIS AND CONFLICT IN EUROPE
The threat perceived?

"YOU KNOW YOU CAN TRUST ME"

◀ The Conservative prime minister, Stanley Baldwin, as portrayed by the British cartoonist David Low in December 1935. Low often reflected the views of left-wing supporters.

▼ The Maginot Line. In fact the German army never attacked the line head on. This picture shows the guns being fired by U.S. army troops against *retreating* German forces in the closing months of World War II.

PACIFISM REMAINED a powerful force in Britain and France in the 1930s. Many people realized that another war would be more devastating than the Great War of 1914–18. In 1932 Stanley Baldwin, who was to be British prime minister from 1935 to 1937, said:

> There is no greater cause of that fear [of war] than the fear of the air . . . it is well for the man in the street to realize that there is no power on earth that can protect him from being bombed . . . the bomber will always get through.[23]

There were many pacifist political groups in Britain, the most famous being the Peace Pledge Union. In October 1937, it had 120,000 members, all committed to this promise:

> We renounce war and never again, either directly or indirectly, will we sanction another.[24]

The threat that Hitler posed to peace was understood in Britain, although people disagreed about how to deal with it. There were three main strands of thought.

Some people believed that Britain should rely on the collective security provided by the League of Nations. This view was widely

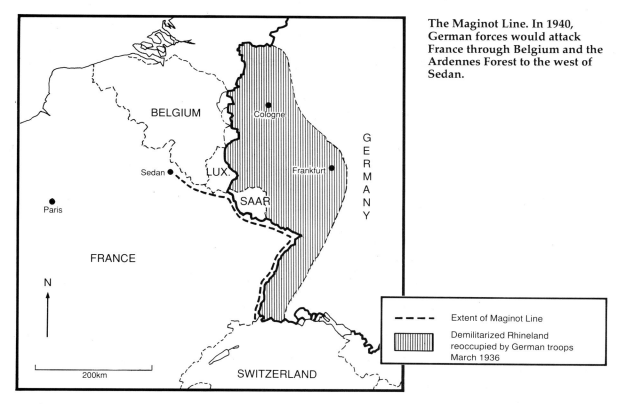

The Maginot Line. In 1940, German forces would attack France through Belgium and the Ardennes Forest to the west of Sedan.

(Map labels: BELGIUM, Cologne, Sedan, LUX., Frankfurt, SAAR, Paris, FRANCE, GERMANY, SWITZERLAND, N, 200km)

Legend:
- – – – Extent of Maginot Line
- Demilitarized Rhineland reoccupied by German troops March 1936

popular among British citizens, at least until 1938, and was the policy supported by the main opposition parties, Labour and the Liberals.

The second view, which was British government policy between 1936 and 1939, sought to give concessions to the German and Italian governments, in the belief that there was a reasonable limit to Hitler's and Mussolini's claims. Some British people thought that Hitler was basically justified in many of his early demands. Neville Chamberlain, the British Conservative prime minister from 1937 to 1940, called this policy "appeasement" and believed, as he wrote in a letter to the Archbishop of Canterbury, that:

[It] alone can save the world from chaos. [25]

As insurance against failure, this policy was accompanied by rearmament, which began seriously in 1936 and speeded up in 1938.

Opposed to this policy of appeasement was a small group of mainly Conservative politicians who believed that the concessions were morally wrong and that Hitler and Mussolini would not stop until challenged. Winston Churchill and Anthony Eden were the most famous adherents of this viewpoint.

In France, pacifism remained strong, and frequent changes of government meant that no firm policy developed toward Germany. The French government was also obstructed by the military strategy adopted by its generals. They had constructed a strong defensive fortification – the Maginot Line – along the Franco-German border. Because of the length and complexity of the Maginot Line, any challenge to Germany had to be accompanied by a declaration of war and a full military draft to man the fortifications. However, the French government would never declare war without outside support – it believed it needed the support of British forces to defeat Germany.

Abyssinia and the Rhineland

By 1934, Mussolini's political position as dictator was strong enough in Italy to allow him to consider a foreign war. The place he chose was Abyssinia – now called Ethiopia – an independent kingdom in East Africa. He had a number of reasons. First, Italy already occupied neighboring Somaliland and Eritrea. Moreover, in 1896 the Abyssinians had inflicted a crushing and embarrassing defeat on Italian troops. Mussolini believed that his forces should now avenge that defeat.

To confront the lightly armed Abyssinian forces, Mussolini sent a large force equipped with modern aircraft and artillery. Italian troops invaded on October 3, 1935, but found the resistance more effective than expected, and it was May 1936 before they occupied Addis Ababa, the Abyssinian capital. A doctor in a field hospital wrote to the League of Nations:

> On January 14, 1936, containers of mustard gas were dropped . . . by the Italian Air Force. Twenty peasants were killed, and I dealt with some fifteen gas cases, two of whom were children.[26]

The Italian government, not surprisingly, denied that gas was being used.

The League of Nations was required by its Covenant to impose economic sanctions against Italy, but these proved ineffective, partly because the British permitted the Italian navy to supply its troops in Abyssinia via the Suez Canal. A secret attempt by Sir Samuel Hoare, the British foreign secretary, and Pierre Laval, the French premier, to grant Italy a portion of Abyssinia was leaked to the press and Hoare resigned. However, worldwide condemnation of Mussolini's action strengthened his political position in Italy. Mussolini's successful invasion demonstrated the weakness of the League and broke the Stresa front that was opposed to German ambitions.

Like Mussolini, Hitler was showing signs of pursuing a more aggressive foreign policy by the mid-1930s. Under the terms of the Treaties of Versailles and Locarno, the Rhineland was a special demilitarized zone of Germany. But on March 7, 1936, a small German force marched peacefully into the Rhineland. Hitler had feared that Britain and France would attack and later admitted:

> If the French had then marched into the Rhineland, we would have had to withdraw without tails between our legs. [27]

This map shows German expansion 1935–9. Each new expansion threatened a neighboring country.

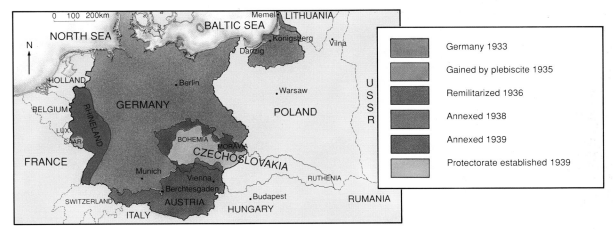

Legend:
- Germany 1933
- Gained by plebiscite 1935
- Remilitarized 1936
- Annexed 1938
- Annexed 1939
- Protectorate established 1939

An Italian propaganda painting of an Italian solider releasing Abyssinian "slaves."

In the event no such action was necessary. French public opinion was uniformly opposed to war. In Britain, the press and most politicians believed Germany was justified in moving troops into its own territory. The French now found it much more difficult to intervene against Germany, and France's will to stand up to German threats was widely doubted. In October 1936, for example, the Belgian government distanced itself from the French by proclaiming itself neutral. It no longer trusted the French to defend it.

A small force of German troops marches into the demilitarized Rhineland. Hitler feared this action would lead to an attack from Britain and France, but in the event they took no measures to stop it.

The Spanish Civil War (1936–9)

Nationalist troops with Republican prisoners in the Spanish Civil War. The fighting caused bitter divisions among Spaniards. Both sides often shot prisoners.

On July 18, 1936, civil war broke out in Spain, between the Republican government and Nationalist rebels. The origins of the war were complex and rooted in the particular circumstances of the country.

The Republican government was supported by some regional governments and the left wing – the socialists, the Communist Party and some anarchists. The Nationalist rebels were army officers supported by the Roman Catholic clergy, monarchists, fascists and other conservatives. When the Nationalists failed to overthrow the government quickly, both sides asked for foreign support.

The war was watched carefully by other European governments. It was the first occasion when fascist and communist states clashed. The Soviet Union intervened on the side of the Republican government, which relied more and more on armaments from the Soviets as the war dragged on. Britain, France and other Western democracies remained neutral. Although the Republican government was democratically elected, the British and French were suspicious of the communists, and their main concern was to be on good terms with whoever won.

The Nationalists, led by General Francisco Franco, received important military support from Italy and Germany. Franco's forces were better armed, organized and disciplined than the Republican forces. When the German government was asked for help by the Nationalist rebels, Hermann Wilhelm Goering, head of the *Luftwaffe* (the German air force), urged Hitler

> . . . *to give support . . . firstly to prevent the further spread of communism; secondly, to test my young* Luftwaffe *in this or that technical respect.*[28]

Goering was most concerned to test the offensive capability of the *Luftwaffe*, for Hitler was building a war machine.

The Spanish Civil War was the first time the Italians and Germans publicly fought on the same side. It drew them together, and by November 1936, Mussolini was talking openly of a "Rome-Berlin Axis," which was made official in 1939.

There were reports of air bombing. A British diplomat visited the small Spanish town of Guernica shortly after it was bombed by German aircraft. He reported:

> To my amazement [I] found that [Guernica], normally of some five thousand inhabitants . . . was almost completely destroyed . . . nine houses in ten are beyond reconstruction.[29]

The artist Pablo Picasso depicted the bombing of this small defenseless town in one of his most famous paintings, "Guernica."

Franco and the Nationalist rebels fought a cautious war against the relatively disorganized Republicans. Offensives were launched only after thorough preparation, and slowly and systematically, the Nationalists won the war. However, although Franco had received support from abroad, during World War II he distanced himself from other fascists, and Spain remained neutral.

A French anti-Nationalist poster after the bombing of Guernica. The text is a quotation from the Bible: "I tell you truly, he who has had this done is not with me but AGAINST me."

Austria and Munich

During World War I, Austria-Hungary had fought with Germany against the Allies. In 1919 Austria's eastern European empire was broken up, and the German-speaking Austrians were forbidden to unite with Germany. The Allies were anxious to prevent Germany from emerging again as the dominant European power. However, Hitler, himself an Austrian, was determined to bring the two countries together. On the very first page of *Mein Kampf*, he had written that "German Austria" must unite itself with the "German Motherland."

The Austrian Nazi Party, funded and directed from Berlin, put pressure on the Austrian government of Chancellor Kurt von Schuschnigg to unite the countries. Von Schuschnigg wanted Austria to remain independent, but he eventually agreed to meet Hitler near Munich on February 12, 1938. Threatening military force, Hitler bullied von Schuschnigg into accepting ten demands, including the appointment of Nazis to the Austrian cabinet. However, when he returned to Austria, von Schuschnigg had second thoughts and called a plebiscite, or referendum. If the people rejected unification, Hitler's claims for Austria could no longer be seen as legitimate.

Hitler was worried by this display of independence and demanded that the plebiscite be postponed. Von Schuschnigg gave in, but too late to prevent German troops from moving across the border. On March 13, Hitler entered Austria's capital, Vienna, to an enthusiastic reception. The British and French governments' protests were halfhearted; Mussolini supported Hitler.

Unofficial British reaction was more hostile. Harold Nicolson, a Member of Parliament, wrote in his diary:

> *Chamberlain (who has the mind and manner of a clothes-brush) aims only at assuring temporary peace at the price of ultimate defeat.* [30]

We, the German Führer and Chancellor and the British Prime Minister, have had a further meeting today and are agreed in recognising that the question of Anglo-German relations is of the first importance for the two countries and for Europe.

We regard the agreement signed last night and the Anglo-German Naval Agreement as symbolic of the desire of our two peoples never to go to war with one another again.

We are resolved that the method of consultation shall be the method adopted to deal with any other questions that may concern our two countries, and we are determined to continue our efforts to remove possible sources of difference and thus to contribute to assure the peace of Europe.

The signatures of Adolf Hitler and Neville Chamberlain on part of the Munich Agreement.

Hitler next turned his attention to Czechoslovakia – a well-armed democracy created in 1919. It was made up of a number of nationalities, as the following table shows:

Czechs	7,447,000
Germans	3,218,000
Slovaks	2,309,000
Magyars	720,000
Ruthenes	569,000
Poles	100,000
Others	266,000

Many of the German-speakers in the Sudetenland (a mountainous region of north and northwest Czechoslovakia) supported the local Nazi Party led by Konrad Henlein. The annexation of Austria caused a large surge in this support, and in March 1938 Hitler encouraged Henlein to demand self-government for the Sudetenland. The Czechoslovakian government of Eduard Beneš strongly opposed this proposal. Self-

On October 10, 1938, enthusiastic Nazis crowded the streets of Asch, near the German-Czech border, to greet Hitler after his troops had occupied the Sudetenland.

government for the German-speakers might have encouraged other minority groups to demand independence, leading to the complete break-up of Czechoslovakia. Moreover, all of Czechoslovakia's strong frontier defenses were in the Sudetenland.

Beneš relied on treaties with the Soviet Union and France to defend him against German aggression and refused to negotiate. However, the support of his allies was far from certain. The Soviet Union would not act alone; the French would need the support of Britain; and Britain did not want war.

On September 15, 1938, Chamberlain flew to Germany for the first of three meetings with Hitler, who at each meeting increased his demands for the Sudentenland. Finally, at Munich on September 29, it was agreed that Hitler could occupy the Sudetenland, and the Czechoslovakian government was forced to give in. This agreement was greeted with great relief in Britain. King George VI wrote to Chamberlain on September 30, 1938:

> I . . . express to you my most heart-felt congratulations on the success of your visit to Munich. [31]

Others disagreed. A British cabinet minister, Duff Cooper, wrote in his diary:

> We listened to the Prime Minister's broadcast . . . It was a most depressing utterance . . . The only sympathy expressed was for Hitler . . . I was furious. [32]

Cooper resigned over this issue.

Chamberlain had expressed sympathy for Hitler and was prepared to appease him in the hope of preventing war.

War is declared

During 1939, the British government reversed its policy of appeasing Hitler. The British public had been horrified by vicious anti-Jewish riots throughout Germany in November 1938. In January 1939, the British government was secretly worried by intelligence, which turned out to be incorrect, that Germany was planning a lightning strike against Britain or France. But the main reason for the change of policy again concerned Czechoslovakia.

Hitler was still determined to destroy Czechoslovakia, and during early 1939 he encouraged Slovak politicians there to claim independence. The Czech government resisted this and became increasingly fearful of German invasion. The Czech president went to Germany to plead with Hitler to spare his country, but Goering threatened to bomb Prague and forced Beneš into submission. On March 15, 1939, German troops were allowed to enter Prague unopposed.

A British biographer of Hitler has written:

> *The message passed, loudly and clearly, to British public opinion: Hitler's notion of diplomacy was to send in his tanks, bully harmless old men, and institute a reign of terror . . . Where would it all end?[33]*

The British government's reacted by giving guarantees to Eastern European countries, which would trigger war if Germany committed further acts of agression. Negotiations followed with Poland, Greece, Turkey, Romania and, most crucially, the Soviet Union.

Stalin recognized Germany as the major threat to the Soviet Union and considered both an alliance with Britain and France to deter Germany and a peace pact with Germany itself. However, the British and French governments seemed to pursue negotiations slowly; British intelligence did not rate Soviet military power highly; Stalin thought Chamberlain a weak and incompetent fool; and military discussions stalled over Poland's refusal to allow Soviet troops onto Polish soil to defend it against Germany. By contrast, secret negotiations between Stalin and Hitler's foreign minister, Joachim von Ribbentrop, proceeded quickly. They concluded with the signing of the Non-Aggression Pact between Germany and the Soviet Union on August 23, 1939. The German officials reported Stalin's comments:

> *The Soviet government takes the new Pact very seriously. He could guarantee on his word of honor that the Soviet Union would not betray its partner.[34]*

The Soviet foreign minister, Molotov, signs the Non-Aggression Pact with Germany. Immediately behind him are Stalin (in uniform) and von Ribbentrop.

The Pact did not alter British or French policy, but it allowed Hitler to attack Poland. Since 1938, he had been urging Poland to let Germany repossess the city of Danzig (now called Gdańsk in Polish), which was Poland's chief port and vital to its economic interests. The city had been controlled since 1920 by the League of Nations and had a large German population. The Polish government, which wrongly believed that its army could contain a German invasion until Britain and France came to help, refused to negotiate. Hitler

A crowd outside 10 Downing Street on September 2, 1939, waiting for the British government's response to the German invasion of Poland.

fixed the invasion date for August 26, 1939. The announcement of a formal treaty between Britain and Poland, and news of Mussolini's reluctance to join Hitler in a European war, only delayed Hitler's invasion plan. On September 1, 1939, German troops crossed the Polish border, and Britain and France, bound by their alliances, declared war on Germany on September 3.

39

5

THE EAST
Japanese militarism

Japanese troops survey captured Chinese firearms after the fall of the Manchurian town of Mukden in 1931.

DURING THE 1920s, a large minority of Japanese people disagreed with the moderate, vaguely pro-Western line followed by most politicians. Many Japanese regretted the disappearance of the old warrior code, whereby

> *Death in the service of one's lord remained the ultimate expression of loyalty.* [35]

These traditionalists worked for a foreign policy aimed at overseas expansion and, in particular, at Japanese control of China.

In the early 1930s, the policies of the expansionists became increasingly popular. The Depression hit Japanese agriculture hard and caused discontent in the countryside, where traditional attitudes had always been strong.

People were also worried by the success of Chiang Kai-shek and the KMT in China, which threatened to prevent Japanese expansion on the mainland. In 1930 there was a political uproar when moderate politicians signed the London Naval Treaty, which imposed restrictions on the power of the Japanese navy.

Expansionist views had strong support in the army and with right-wing extremists. There was a growth of extreme political societies, which were responsible for the assassinations of some senior politicians.

Since 1906 the Japanese troops had been stationed in South Manchuria, a region of northeast China, to protect the assets they had won in the war against Russia. The commanders of this force, known as the Kwantung army, were very sympathic to the expansion-

The Japanese emperor blesses soldiers at a temple in Tokyo before they leave for the war in China in 1937.

ist case. Acting without the approval of the Japanese government, they decided to invade the rest of Manchuria. They needed an excuse; therefore, on September 18, 1931, they blew up the railroad line they were supposed to be guarding and blamed the explosion on the Chinese. By January 1932, ignoring the half-hearted protests of the civilian government in Tokyo, the Kwantung army controlled Manchuria and was fighting Chinese troops on Chinese soil.

The reaction of the international community was muted. The United States disapproved of the action and refused to recognize any land gained by the Japanese. China appealed to the League of Nations, which sent a commission of inquiry. It reported in October 1932 and was very critical of the Japanese invasion. In the face of this international criticism, Japan withdrew from the League in March 1933, and Japanese public opinion united behind the Kwantung army's action.

The Japanese prime minister, Hideki Tojo (in uniform, front row), with his 1941 war cabinet. Tojo was a major influence on Japanese politics in the 1930s. He favored a policy of aggressive expansionism for Japan.

Japan and China at war

▲ Japanese troops attack the northern railroad station of the Chinese city of Shanghai.

◄ A Chinese Nationalist poster of 1938 portrays efficient KMT resistance to the advancing Japanese troops.

The Manchurian invasion met with widespread approval in Japan, and the moderate politicians who argued against a policy of expansionism became more and more unpopular. The moderate prime minister, Inukai Tsuyoshi, was murdered by extremists, some of them army cadets, on May 15, 1932. His place was taken by an admiral, and from then on Japanese politics were increasingly dictated by groups within the armed forces.

In February 1936 one of these groups, called the *Kodo* (or "imperial way"), tried to seize power. They failed but were soon replaced by another group of army officers called *Tosei* ("control"), who wanted to establish a dictatorship that would be powerful enough to take Japan into a major war. The war they wanted started in China in July 1937 and went on until the defeat of Japan by the Allies in 1945.

Ever since the invasion of Manchuria, there had been occasional fighting between the Kwantung army and Chiang Kai-shek's forces in northern China. On the night of July 7, 1937, they clashed at the Marco Polo Bridge, near Peking. Chiang Kai-shek had recently restored his friendship with the Soviet Union, which was worried by Japanese ambitions. This Soviet support may have given the KMT confidence to resist the Japanese more strongly than usual. However, the Japanese used the resistance to justify a full-scale

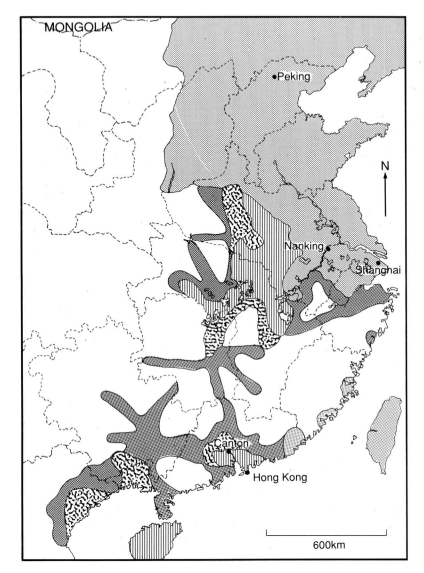

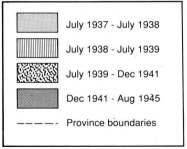

░░░	July 1937 - July 1938
‖‖‖	July 1938 - July 1939
∴∴∴	July 1939 - Dec 1941
▓▓▓	Dec 1941 - Aug 1945
— — —	Province boundaries

This map demonstrates how difficult it was for the Japanese troops to extend their control away from the cities and lines of communication in southern China.

assault on China. They believed that it would be easy to conquer the whole country. Peking fell quickly. The rest of China did not.

During the autumn of 1937, Japan engaged in widespread air bombing of civilian targets. By December Japanese troops had captured the Nationalist capital Nanking, where they carried out atrocities, murdering, raping and looting. Japan paid no attention to increasing international disapproval, and on December 12, 1937, Japanese aircraft even attacked the USS *Panay*, an American gunboat on the Yangtze River. However, the United States did not retaliate, and in the end, the Japanese government apologized.

As a result of international disapproval, Japan tried to improve its relations with Germany. In 1936 the two countries had signed the Anti-Comintern Pact, which contained a secret defensive alliance against the Soviet Union. During 1938, Japan tried unsuccessfully to negotiate for a closer alliance.

Japan and the Soviet Union

Japanese troops preparing for battle with Soviet troops on the border at Changkufeng.

The Soviet Union remained hostile to Japan throughout the 1930s. In part, the Soviets worried that the Japanese invasion of Manchuria would be extended, not southward into China, but northward into the Soviet Union. The Soviets also feared Japanese hostility to communism. In 1935 the seventh Congress of the Comintern had identified Germany, Italy and Japan as the main threats to communism and world peace. The Anti-Comintern Pact in 1936 seemed to confirm this view.

When Japan attacked China, the Soviet Union supported Chiang Kai-shek. Relations between Japan and the Soviet Union worsened. By July 1938, tension was high on the long border between Japanese-occupied territory and the Soviet Union. The local people were reported to have said:

The Kwantung army is a tiger in the south but a pussycat in the north . . .[36]

But as one senior officer put it, the Japanese army was, in fact, telling the Soviets:

Take another step and we'll let you have it.[36]

Fighting eventually broke out on the border at Chang-KuFeng. A ceasefire was arranged, but both sides were dissatisfied with the compromise, and a year later fighting broke out again in Mongolia. This time, Stalin sent a previously unknown general, Georgy Zhukov, who carefully brought together his tanks, infantry and aircraft in a massive offensive on August 20, 1939, which destroyed the Japanese forces. Although this attack was so successful, it received very little attention in the West and did not alter European assumptions that the Red Army was weak.

The Kwantung army's defeat made Japan wary of a full-scale war against the Soviet Union. The Nazi-Soviet Non-Aggression

Georgy Zhukov (wearing the sash) photographed in Berlin at the end of World War II. On his left is British Field Marshal Montgomery.

Pact, signed three days later to Japan's great surprise, meant that any immediate hope of an alliance with Germany had also disappeared. In China, Japanese forces were still fighting Chiang Kai-shek, and a major Chinese attack in the winter of 1939–40 made a long war look likely. Japan's position did not seem to be particularly strong. However, the outbreak of war in Europe was to give the Japanese some unexpected opportunities.

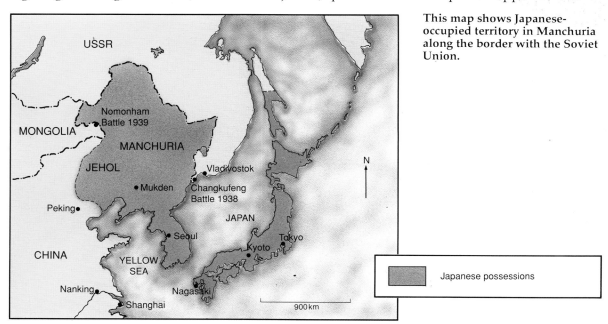

This map shows Japanese-occupied territory in Manchuria along the border with the Soviet Union.

6

FROM WAR TO WORLD WAR
The end of U.S. isolationism

A convoy of twenty-four British ships. In 1941 the U.S. Navy began to protect British convoys from German submarines in the western Atlantic.

FOR MOST OF THE 1930s, isolationism remained a dominant aspect of American foreign policy. If anything, the economic problems caused by the Depression led Americans to concentrate more closely on their own affairs and to ignore the international scene. Franklin D. Roosevelt, elected president in 1932, did not want to damage his popularity by challenging this mood. He did, however, appoint Cordell Hull as secretary of state. Hull believed strongly that international cooperation would reduce the chance of war.

The strength of isolationism was shown by the Neutrality Acts, the first of which came into force in 1935. Under these laws, the United States would refuse to sell or supply arms to any country at war, regardless of whether it sympathized with that country's cause. Isolationists supported this law because they believed that Europe would certainly go to war again. They believed it was

best to remain neutral. Those politicians who disagreed – the internationalists, such as Henry L. Stimson (Hull's predecessor as secretary of state) – believed:

> *The only certain way to keep out of a great war is to prevent that war taking place.* [37]

People like Hull and Stimson thought that the United States should support the collective security provided by the League of Nations.

As the American public watched Hitler's repeated aggression in Europe, Roosevelt felt able to move away from an isolationist position. In October 1937 he said:

> *The peace, the freedom and the security of 90 percent of the population of the world is being jeopardized by the remaining 10 percent.* [38]

Although the government and people still wanted to stay out of any European war, when war did break out most Americans sympathized with Britain and France. The defeat of France in the spring of 1940 alarmed many Americans. Expenditure on rearmament rose quickly, and in September 1940 the United States agreed that Britain could buy fifty old American destroyers.

Roosevelt fought a presidential election campaign in late 1940, and although the opposing Republican Party candidate, Wendell L. Willkie, agreed with Roosevelt's support for the British, the vocal "America First" organization made sure that the isolationist cause got full publicity. When Roosevelt won, he found a way to increase aid to Britain. Knowing that by June 1941 Britain would run out of money, he proposed in January 1941 that war materials would be "loaned" to Britain for the duration of the war. In April 1941, he ordered the U.S. navy to protect convoys on their way to Britain. U.S. Marines were stationed in Greenland and then in Iceland. Even now, however, the United States was still not at war.

▲ On September 25, 1940, Roosevelt signed the act of Congress that authorized the U.S. armed forces to draft men between the ages of twenty and thirty-five for military service.

◀ American volunteer recruits to the British army undergo basic training in England.

Barbarossa

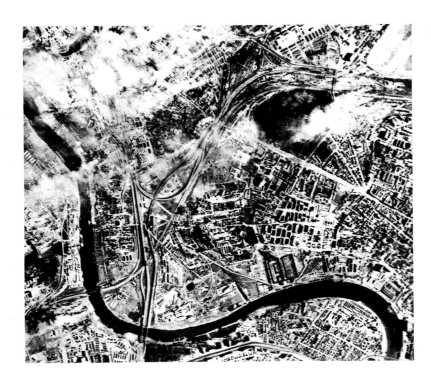

Moscow, seen from a German bomber in August 1941.

Having defeated Poland in 1939, German forces attacked and occupied Denmark, Norway, the Netherlands, Belgium and much of France in the Spring of 1940. Britain refused to negotiate and resisted an attempt by the German air force to prepare the way for a possible invasion. However, instead of continuing to attack Britain, Hitler decided in December 1940 to launch Operation Barbarossa – an attack on the Soviet Union.

Why did Hitler attack the Soviet Union? There were many good reasons not to do so. It meant fighting on two fronts, particularly if the United States joined the war on Britain's side. The Soviet Union was a vast country, and even if its capital, Moscow, were captured, there were hundreds of miles of land farther east. German forces relied on fast movement by tanks and aircraft, and they would have difficulty coordinating an effective attack. Moreover, in June 1940, Italy had joined the war on Germany's side and already needed help with its campaigns in Greece and North Africa.

Hitler maintained that it was sensible to invade the Soviet Union. He gave two reasons for Operation Barbarossa to his secretary, Martin Bormann, in 1945:

> Britain . . . under the guidance of its stupid chiefs, would have refused to recognize the hegemony [dominance] we set up in Europe as long as there remained on the continent a great power which was fundamentally hostile to [Germany] . . . We had another reason . . . it was absolutely certain that one day or other [the Soviet Union] would attack us.[39]

There were probably other reasons for the attack. From the 1920s onward, Hitler repeatedly referred to his ambition to create a vast empire in Eastern Europe. If he were to succeed, he would have to defeat the Soviet Union sooner or later. But Stalin was rearming his country fast, and, at that time, Germany was not economically strong enough for a long war. Hitler believed in 1940

48

that the Soviet armed forces were still weak and would quickly submit to those of Germany. This belief was shared by many people, including the British Secret Intelligence Service. It had been reinforced by a war in the winter of 1939–40, when the Soviet Union had attacked Finland and defeated that small country only with difficulty. Few people had paid attention to or remembered Zhukhov's success against the Japanese in 1939.

During 1940 and 1941, Germany and the Soviet Union quarreled over various parts of Eastern Europe, notably Bessarabia (an oil-producing area of Romania) and Bulgaria. In early 1941, Stalin had early information that the Germans might attack. In May, Stalin's intelligence service reported from eastern Germany:

> *German officers and men speak with complete frankness about the coming war between Germany and the Soviet Union.*[40]

Britain and the United States warned Stalin of Hitler's plans, but he ignored them. He suspected them of trying to break up the Nazi-Soviet Pact. To avoid inciting a German attack, he refused to mobilize the Red Army, so the Soviet Union was militarily unprepared for the German assault when it began on June 22, 1941.

▶ **A Soviet airfield is bombed by German ground-attack aircraft.**

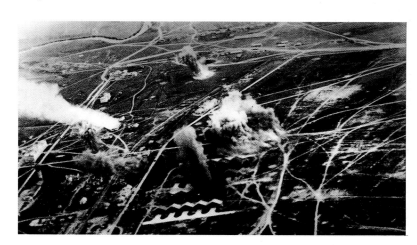

▼ **German horse-drawn transport bypasses a disabled Soviet tank in the early days of Operation Barbarossa.**

Pearl Harbor

As the war in China proceeded, the United States had become increasingly unfriendly toward Japan. In October 1939, the U.S. ambassador to Japan said the American people

> . . . have good reason to believe that an effort is being made to establish control, in Japan's own interest, of large areas of . . . Asia and . . . added to the effect of the bombings . . . that accounts for the attitude of the American people. [41]

By the summer of 1940, the occupation of the Netherlands, the defeat of France and Britain's embattled position meant that these European countries could not defend their Far Eastern colonies. On September 19, 1940, Japan announced that it considered these col-onies to be part of a future Japanese empire, the "Greater East Asian Co-Prosperity Sphere." On September 27, 1940, Japan entered into a Tripartite Pact with Germany and Italy to ensure that if the United States entered the war against either Germany or Japan, the other two countries would, in turn, declare war on the United States.

During 1940, the United States applied economic pressure on Japan, preventing the export of war materials and aviation fuel. During early 1941, discussions took place between Japan and the United States. The Japanese wanted the United States to make Chiang Kai-shek give in, and the United States wanted the Japanese to withdraw from China. The talks failed. In July 1941, Japanese troops landed in French Indochina, and the

Two U.S. battleships, one sunk and one on fire, after the Japanese attack on Pearl Harbor.

50

United States imposed a ban on all trade with Japan.

In Japan itself, the army's attitude became more uncompromising, and in October 1941 the Japanese government decided that war with the United States was inevitable. The extremely militant General Hideki Tojo was appointed prime minister on October 18, and plans for a surprise attack on the U.S. Naval Base at Pearl Harbor in Hawaii were immediately put into action. President Roosevelt and his advisers had reliable warnings of an attack but did not expect it there. The attack on December 7, 1941, which coincided with a Japanese declaration of war on the United States, was devastating.

Four days later, in accordance with assurances previously given to Japan, and knowing that the United States would now enter the war on Britain's side, Hitler declared war on the United States. The British prime minister, Winston Churchill, wrote:

These gangs and cliques of wicked men and their military or party organizations have been able to bring these hideous evils upon mankind. It would indeed bring shame upon our generation if we did not teach them a lesson which will not be forgotten in the records of a thousand years. [42]

Germany, Italy and Japan were now at war with the Allies led by Britain, the United States and the Soviet Union. With the entry of the United States and Japan, the war had become even more of a worldwide conflict than that which had erupted only a quarter of a century before.

A Dutch anti-Japanese poster. The slogan reads: "The Indies [the Dutch colonies in the Far East] must be free! Work and fight for that!"

An American recruiting poster encouraging men who had not yet been compulsorily drafted to join the armed forces as volunteers.

51

Leading figures

Colonel Josef Beck (1894–1944)
Polish foreign minister 1932–9.
He was a soldier, then a diplomat, before turning to politics. He negotiated a pact with Britain in 1939.

Eduard Beneš (1884–1948)
President of Czechoslovakia 1935–8.
He became the foreign minister of the new state of Czechoslovakia in 1918 and was a strong supporter of the League of Nations. He resigned over the Munich agreement, which he believed to be a disgrace for his country.

Aristide Briand (1862–1932)
French foreign minister.
In 1927 he proposed that there should be a treaty outlawing war. This, the Kellogg-Briand Pact, was signed in 1928. He was socialist prime minister of France for eleven separate terms between 1909 and 1929.

Neville Chamberlain (1869–1940)
British prime minister 1937–40.
He entered Parliament in 1918 and became Conservative chancellor of the exchequer in 1931. He had little knowledge of foreign affairs and, between 1936 and 1939, pursued a policy of appeasing Hitler and Mussolini.

Winston Leonard Spencer Churchill (1874–1965)
British prime minister 1940–45 and 1951–55.
Born into a rich and powerful English family, he was a soldier and journalist before entering Parliament in 1900. He held various senior government posts, including the chancellorship of the exchequer between 1924 and 1929. A skilled parliamentary speaker, in the late 1930s he loudly opposed government policy of appeasement and urged faster rearmament. He was reappointed naval minister in September 1939 and succeeded Chamberlain as prime minister in May 1940.

Representatives at the Paris Peace Conference (left to right): Lloyd George, Orlando, Clemenceau and Woodrow Wilson.

Count Galeazzo Ciano (1903–44)
Italian foreign minister 1936–43.
A fascist, he married Mussolini's daughter, and was an air force pilot in Abyssinia in 1935. He first supported, and later sought to oppose, the alliance with Nazi Germany.

Georges Clemenceau (1841–1929)
French prime minister.
A vicious debater and powerful journalist, Clemenceau was first appointed to government office in 1906. He was prime minister 1906–09, and again 1917–20. He was fiercely patriotic and anti-German and negotiated the Treaty of Versailles in 1919.

(Robert) Anthony Eden (1897–1977)
British foreign secretary 1935–8.
He entered Parliament in 1923, as a member of the Conservative Party, and was continuously interested in foreign affairs. A strong

With the help of Germany and Italy, Franco (center) led the Nationalist rebels to victory during the Spanish Civil War.

supporter of the League of Nations, he resigned in February 1938 because he disagreed with Chamberlain's policy of appeasing Mussolini. Broadly speaking, he supported Churchill's attacks on government policy.

Francisco Franco (Y Bahamonde) (1892–1975).
"Caudillo" (leader) of Spain, 1939–75.
Leader of rebel Nationalist forces in the Spanish Civil War. A soldier, he was chief of the army high command in 1935, but was sent to be Governor of the Canary Islands immediately before the revolution in 1936. His forces eventually overcame the Republican armies in the Civil War (in 1939), and Franco became Caudillo of Spain.

Joseph Stalin, dictator of the Soviet Union. In 1939, Stalin and Hitler signed a Non-Aggression Pact, which kept the Soviet Union out of the war until June 1941, when it was invaded by the German army.

Adolf Hitler (1889–1945)

German dictator 1933–45.

Born in Austria, he served as a soldier in the German army in World War I. A skilled public speaker, Hitler built up the Nazi Party to be a national political force by 1930 and was appointed chancellor in 1933. He became Führer (leader) of Germany in 1934. His policies of rearmament, economic development and confrontation with foreign countries resulted in so powerful a German state that it took the combined forces of the United States, the Soviet Union, Britain and the other Allies until May 1945 to defeat it. Hitler shot himself in April 1945 when it was obvious that Germany had lost the war.

Cordell Hull (1871–1955)

U.S. secretary of state 1933–44.

He was born in Tennessee and entered Congress in 1907. He was a strong supporter of "internationalism" (that is, anti-isolationism) and believed that import duties led to economic development and the promotion of international peace.

Vladimir Ilyich Lenin (1870–1924)

Soviet leader, 1917–24.

The first premier of the Soviet Union, Lenin's original surname was Ulyanov. He formed the Bolsheviks in 1903 and led them in the October Revolution (1917), which established the Soviet goverment. He formed the Comintern in 1919.

David Lloyd George (1863–1945)

British prime minister, 1916–22.

He grew up in Wales, entered Parliament in 1890, as a member of the Liberal Party, and served as chancellor of the exchequer between 1908 and 1915. He was prime minister when the Treaty of Versailles was drawn up.

Benito Mussolini (1883–1945).

Italian prime minister 1922–43.

The son of a blacksmith, he was a soldier and journalist before setting up the Italian fascist party in 1919. He became head of government in 1922 and pursued policies of economic development, increasing dictatorship and foreign aggression. Mussolini's Italy sided with Germany in 1936 but did not enter World War II until June 1940, when he thought Hitler was about to win.

Joachim von Ribbentrop (1893–1946)
German foreign minister 1938–45.
He was a soldier, wine merchant and Nazi before being Nazi Party foreign affairs spokesman between 1933 and 1936. He was German ambassador in London 1936–8.

Franklin Delano Roosevelt (1882–1945)
President of the United States 1933–45.
He was a lawyer before entering politics in 1911. He was crippled by polio in 1921 but was elected president as a Democrat in 1932, winning forty-two states against his opponents' six. Concerned mainly with economic recovery between 1933 and 1940, he engaged seriously in foreign affairs only after World War II had begun.

Josef Vissarionovich Stalin (1879–1953)
General Secretary of the Communist Party of the Soviet Union 1922–53.
Born J. V. Djugashvili, he changed his name ("Stalin" means "of steel") to evade the police. He was a revolutionary from his youth onward, eventually succeeded Lenin as the most powerful man in the Soviet Union and made himself dictator. He was largely ignorant about foreign affairs during the early years of his dictatorship.

Gustav Stresemann (1878–1929)
German foreign minister 1923–9.
Stresemann was a moderate but strongly nationalistic politician, who constructed and led the policy of rehabilitating Germany into the world community.

Hideki Tojo (1884–1948)
Japanese prime minister 1941–4.
A soldier and distinguished general, he was a major influence on Japanese politics in the 1930s, arguing in favor of an aggressive expansionist policy for Japan. He was appointed war minister in 1940.

Wilson, twenty-eighth president of the United States, led his country into World War I in 1917 and secured the formation of the League of Nations in 1919.

Leon Trotsky (1879–1940)
A Russian revolutionary and communist theorist, he was a leader of the Revolution in 1917. As commissar of foreign affairs and war (1917–24), he was largely responsible for creating the Red Army. He was ousted by Stalin after Lenin's death and deported from Russia in 1929. He was assassinated by a Stalinist agent in 1940.

(Thomas) Woodrow Wilson (1856–1924)
President of the United States 1913–21.
He was a lawyer and university professor before entering politics in 1910. He kept the United States out of World War I until 1917; its intervention was then decisive. After the war, the League of Nations owed its very existence to this idealistic man.

Important dates

Date	Events

Date   **Events**

1914–18   World War I.

1918   *November 11* The armistice is signed.

1919   *January–June* The Paris Peace Conference.
March 18 The formation of the Comintern.
June 28 The Treaty of Versailles is signed.

1920   *March 19* The U.S. Senate finally refuses to accept the Treaty of Versailles.

1921   *November 14* The Washington Naval Conference on Asian and Pacific affairs.

1922   *October 28* Mussolini marches on Rome. He becomes Italian prime minister.

1923   *January 11* Following the German failure to pay reparations, French and Belgian troops occupy the Ruhr.
September 1 Italian troops occupy Corfu.
November 8–9 Hitler attempts to seize power in Munich.

1924   *January 21* Lenin dies.
April 1 Hitler is sentenced to five years' imprisonment. He writes *Mein Kampf* while in prison.
September 1 The Dawes Plan is put into operation.

1925   *December 1* The Treaty of Locarno is signed. Germany is admitted to the League of Nations.

1926   Stalin takes control in the Soviet Union.
Chiang Kai-shek takes over the Kuomintang.
September 9 Germany joins the League of Nations.

1927   *April* Chiang Kai-shek orders the massacre of local Chinese communits.

1927–8   The Kuomintang and Japanese troops clash.

1929   *October 24* The Wall Street Crash.

1930   *September 14* The first electoral success for the Nazis.

1931   *September 18* The Japanese army invades Manchuria.

1932   *May 15* The Japanese prime minister is murdered.

1933   *January 30* Hitler is appointed chancellor of Germany.
German rearmament begins.
March 27 Japan leaves the League of Nations.
May 16 The United States formally recognizes the Soviet Union.
July 14 Hitler bans non-Nazi parties.
October 14 Germany leaves the League of Nations.

1934   *September 18* The Soviet Union joins the League of Nations.

1935   *August 31* The first Neutrality Act comes into force in the United States. The Acts strengthen the U.S. policy of isolationism.
October 2 Italy invades Abyssinia.

1936   *February 29* A military coup fails in Japan.
March 7 Germany invades the Rhineland.
July 18 The start of the Spanish Civil War.
November 25 Anti-Comintern Pact.

1937   *July 7* The outbreak of war between Japan and China.

1938   *March 13* Germany forcibly reunites with Austria.
July 24 Fighting breaks out between the Soviet Union and Japan.
April–September The Czechoslovakian crisis.

Date	Events
1938	*September 29* Chamberlain agrees that Hitler may occupy the Sudetenland (the Munich agreement).
1939	*March 15* Germany takes control in Czechoslovakia.
	April 1 End of the Spanish Civil War.
	August 23 A Non-Agression Pact between Germany and the Soviet Union is signed.
	September 1 Germany invades Poland.
	September 3 Britain and France declare war on Germany.
1940	*April 9–May 10* Germany attacks Denmark, Norway, the Netherlands, Belgium and France.
	June 10 Italy enters the war as Germany's ally.
	September 27 Tripartite Pact between Germany, Japan and Italy.
1941	The United States begins to support Britain without entering war.
	June 22 Germany attacks the Soviet Union.
	July 26 Japan invades French Indochina. The United States bans trade with Japan.
	December 7 Japan attacks the U.S. fleet at Pearl Harbor.
	December 11 Hitler declares war on the United States.
1945	*May 8* Germany surrenders.
	August 14 Japan surrenders.

Glossary

Armistice	A truce or ceasefire.
Axis	An alliance between a number of states to coordinate their foreign policy.
Bolsheviks	Members of the Russian Communist Party who seized power in October 1917.
Chancellor	In Germany, the prime minister.
Chancellor of the exchequer	In Britain, the cabinet minister responsible for finance.
Coalition	An agreement between states or political parties to act together.
Collective security	A policy of mutual protection, as when states act together to stop armed aggression against one or more of their number.
Colony	A territory that is dependent upon, and ruled by, a small number of people from another state.
Comintern	An organization set up by the Bolsheviks in 1919 to encourage revolution abroad. It is also called the "Third International."
Communist	A person who believes in the abolition of private property, the state control of industry and the creation of a classless society.
Constitution	The set of basic rules by which a state is governed.
Decree	An order or law issued by someone in authority.
Delegation	A group of representatives at a conference.
Democracy	A nation governed by elected representatives.
Depression	The cycle of reduced economic output, reduced prices, a weakened banking system and increasing unemployment.
Dictatorship	Absolute government, usually by one person.
Economic output	The total goods and services produced by a country.
Empire	The peoples and territories under the rule of a single state.
Expansionism	The doctrine of expanding the economy or territory of a country.
Fascist	A person who favors right-wing dictatorship, expansionism and anti-communism, such as that practiced by Mussolini.
Holocaust	The murder of millions of Jews by the Nazis.
Import duties	Government taxes on imported goods.
Inflation	A progressive increase in the general level of prices.
Isolationism	A policy of not taking part in foreign affairs.
Left-wing policy	Political ideas that advocate radical political, social and economic changes, and aim to achieve greater equality.
Militancy	Aggressiveness in support of a political cause.
Monarchist	Someone who favors a form of government in which supreme authority is vested in a king or queen.
Nationalist	Someone who believes in, or strives for, the unity, independence, interests or expansion of a nation composed of people who share the same language, culture and history.
Nazi	A follower of Hitler and his policies of German nationalism, expansionism, dictatorship and hatred of Jewish people.
October Revolution	The second revolution in Russia in 1917, in which the Bolsheviks seized power from the democratic provisional government, which itself had taken over from the old imperial government in February that year.
Pacifist	Someone who believes that war is wrong in all circumstances.
Pact	An agreement or treaty between states.

Plebiscite	A referendum. The direct vote by the people of a country on a question of national importance.
Premier	The head of a government.
Proletariat	The lower or working class.
Propaganda	The organized use of a mixture of truth and lies to win people over to a particular point of view.
Rearmament	The building up of stocks of weapons and military force in preparation for war.
Reichstag	The German parliament.
Reparations	The fines paid by the losing side after a war.
Ruhr	The main industrial and mining area of western Germany.
Secret diplomacy	Making alliances, pacts and treaties in secret.
Self-determination	The right of a nation or people to determine its own form of government, or to decide to which state they should belong.
Socialism	The belief that the community, rather than individuals, should control the means of economic output.
Stock market	A market where shares in companies and some other financial assets are traded.
Traditionalist	Someone who thinks things should be done the way they have been done in the past.
Treaty	A formal agreement between states.
Tripartite	Consisting of three parts or involving three participants.
Unification	Bringing together or joining separate things.
Wall Street Crash	The collapse of share price on the New York Stock Exchange on October 24, 1929.

Further reading

Hacker, Jeffrey H. *Franklin D. Roosevelt* (Franklin Watts, 1983)
Harris, Sarah. *How and Why: The Second World War* (David & Charles, 1989)
Leckie, Robert. *Story of World War II* (Random House, 1964)
Messenger, Charles. *The Second World War* (Franklin Watts, 1987)
Shapiro, William E. *Pearl Harbor* (Franklin Watts, 1984)

Picture acknowledgments

The author and publishers would like to thank the following for allowing their illustrations to be used in this book: Hulton Picture Company 46; Imperial War Museum 5 (bottom), 13, 23, 27 (bottom), 28, 29 (top), 33 (bottom), 36, 38, 41 (bottom), 45 (top), 47, 48, 49 (both), 50, 51 (both); Mary Evans Picture Library *cover*, 5 (top), 7, 11 (bottom), 15 (top), 22, 24, 29 (bottom), 34, 42 (top), 52, 53, 54; Popperfoto 9 (bottom), 11 (top) 18, 25, 26, 37, 39; Punch 6, 8; Topham 9 (top), 10, 15 (bottom), 16, 20, 21 (both), 30 (both), 33 (top), 35, 40, 41 (top), 42 (bottom), 44, 47 (top), 55. All other pictures are from the Wayland Picture Library. The artwork was supplied by Brian Davey.

Notes on sources

1 Keynes, John Maynard, *The Economic Consequences of the Peace*, Macmillan: Royal Economic Society, 1971, p. 142. Originally published in 1919.
2 Joyce, James Avery, *Broken Star: The Story of the League of Nations*, Christopher Davies, 1978, p. 22.
3 Ibid, p. 64.
4 Bemis, S.F., "Washington's Farewell Address" in *American Historical Review 39*, (1934). The address was delivered in 1796.
5 McCoy, Donald R., *Calvin Coolidge*, Macmillan, 1967, p. 190.
6 De Santis, Vincent P., *A History of United States Foreign Policy*, (4th ed), Prentice Hall, 1980, p. 290.
7 Bell, P.M.H., *The Origins of the Second World War in Europe*, Longman, 1986, p. 12.
8 Roskill, Stephen, *Hankey: Man of Secrets*, Vol. 2, Collins, 1974, pp. 149–50.
9 Lyttelton, Adrian (ed.), *Italian Fascisms*, Cape, 1973, p. 315.
10 *Ibid.* p. 47.
11 Lenin, V.I., *Collected Works* Vol. 24, Lawrence & Wishart, 1963–70, pp. 21–6.
12 Deutscher, Isaac, *The Prophet Unarmed*, OUP, 1959, p. 301.
13 Jansen, Marius B., *Japan and China: From War to Peace 1894–1972*, Rand McNally, 1975, p. 338.
14 Quoted in Ulam, Adam B, *Expansion and Co-existence: Soviet Foreign Policy 1917–73*, (2nd ed), Frederick E. Praeger, 1973, p. 177.
15 De Jonge, Alec, *The Weimar Chronicle*, Paddington Press, 1978, p. 97.
16 Gordon, Harold J., *The Reichswehr and the German Republic 1919–26*, Princeton University Press, 1957, p. 247.
17 Gebhardt, Bruno, *Handbuch der Deutschen Geschichte*, Union Verlag, 1959, p. 352.
18 Bracher, Karl Dietrich, *The German Dictatorship*, Peregrine, 1978, p. 248.
19 Noakes, J. and Pridham, G., *Documents on Nazism 1919–45*, Jonathan Cape, 1974.
20 Churchill, Winston S., *The Second World War* Vol. 1, The Reprint Society, 1950, p. 61.
21 Hitler, Adolf, *Mein Kampf*, (ed. James Murphy), Hurst & Blackwood, 1939, p. 509.
22 Baynes, Norman H., *The Speeches of Adolf Hitler*, OUP, 1942, p. 1107.
23 *Parliamentary Debates: Official Report* 5th Series, Vol. 270/632, House of Commons, November 10, 1932.
24 Deadel, Martin, *Pacifism in Britain 1914–1945*, Clarendon Press, 1980.
25 Feiling, Keith, *Life of Neville Chamberlain*, Macmillan, 1946, p. 375.
26 Del Boca, Algelo, *The Ethiopian War 1935–41*, Chicago, 1969, p. 83.
27 Schimdt, Paul, *Hitler's Interpreter*, William Heinemann, 1951, p. 41.
28 Thomas, Hugh, *The Spanish Civil War*, (3rd ed), Hamish Hamilton, 1977, p. 355.
29 Quoted in Thomas, Hugh, *The Spanish Civil War*, (3rd ed), Hamish Hamilton, 1977, p. 986.
30 Nicolson, Harold, *Diary and Letters 1930–39*, (ed. Nigel Nicolson), Collins, 1966, p. 345.
31 Feiling, Keith, *Life of Neville Chamberlain*, Macmillain, 1946, p. 378.
32 Cooper, Duff, *Old Men Forget*, Rupert Hart-Davis, 1953, p. 238.
33 Stone, Norman, *Hitler*, Hodder & Stoughton, 1980, p. 88.
34 *Documents on German Foreign Policy: 1918–1945*, Series D, Vol. 7, HMSO, 1956, p. 229.
35 Beasley, W.G., *The Modern History of Japan*, Weidenfeld & Nicolson, 1981, p. 7.
36 Cook, Alvin D., *The Anatomy of a Small War*, Greenwood Press, 1977.
37 Divine, Robert A., *The Reluctant Belligerent*, John Wiley, 1965.
38 Roosevelt, Franklin D., *The Public and Addresses*, Macmillan, 1941, p. 410.
39 Bormann, Martin, *The Testament of Adolf Hitler*, Cassell, 1961, p. 64.
40 Erickson, John, *The Road of Stalingrad*, Weidenfeld & Nicolson, 1975, p. 87.
41 Quoted in De Santis, Vincent P., *A History of United States Foreign Policy*, (4th ed), Prentice Hall, 1980, p. 348.
42 Churchill, Winston S., *The Second World War*, Vol. 3, Cassell, 1950, p. 488.

Index

Figures in **bold** refer to illustrations

Abyssinia 32
Albania 13
Allies 4, 36, 42, 51
Alsace-Lorraine 5
Anti-Comintern Pact 43
anti-Semitism 27, 28, 38
Austria 36
Austria-Hungary 4, 36

Baldwin, Stanley 30
Barbarossa 48–9
Beck, Colonel Joseph 52
Belgium 11, 22, 33, 48
Beneš, Eduard 36, 52
Bolshevism 13, 14
Bormann, Martin 48
Briande, Aristide **7**, 9, 52
Britain 4, 7, 8, 9, 10, 11, 13, 16, 17, 20, 21, 32, 33,
    34, 36, 37, 38, 39, 47, 48, 50, 51
    alliances 11, 17
    concessions to Germany 31
    concessions to Italy 31
    declaration of war 39
    defense spending 10
    pacifism 30
    rearmament 7, 31
Brüning, Heinrich 24, 25, 26

Chamberlain, Neville 31, 37, 52, 53
    policy of appeasement 31, 38, 52
Chang-KuFeng, battle at 44, **44**
China 17, 18–19, 40, 41, 44, 45
    nationalism 19
    revolution 18
    treaties 18
    war with Japan 19, 42–3, 50
Churchill, Winston 10, **10**, 28, 31, 51, 52, 53
Clemenceau, Georges 4, 10, 52, **53**
Comintern 14, 44
Coolidge, Calvin 9, **9**
Czechoslovakia 36–7, 38

Danzig (Gdańsk) 39
Dawes Plan 20, 23
Denmark 48
Depression 20–21, 27, 40, 46

economic boom, 1920s 20
Eden, Anthony 31, 53

Far East 16, 18, 40–41, 42–3, 44–5
fascism 13, 34
Finland 49
France 7, 8, 9, 10, 11, 13, 16, 17, 21, 22, 32, 33, 34,
    37, 38, 39, 47
    declaration of war 39
    defeat by Germany 47, 48, 50
    occupation of Ruhr 11, **11**, 22
    pacifism 10, 30, 31
    rearmament 7
Franco, General Francisco 34, 35, 53, **53**

Gdańsk (*see Danzig*)
Germany 4, 5, 7, 8, 22–3, 24, 25, 31, 34, 36, 38, 51
    and Czechoslovakia 36–7, 38
    armed forces 4, 5, 32, 34, 35, 36, 47, 48
    attack on Poland 39, 48
    attack on Soviet Union 48–9
    defeat of France by 47, 48, 50
    dislike of Treaty of Versailles 5, 22, 23, 24
    economy 22, 27
    elections 24
    expansionism 28, 36, 38, 39, 48
    inflation 22, 24
    invasion of Austria 36
    nationalism 23
    occupation of Belgium, Denmark, Norway,
        and the Netherlands 48
    occupation of Sudetenland 36–7
    pact with Japan 43
    pack with Soviet Union 38–9, **38**, 44
    rearmament 27, 28–9
    reparations 4, 5, 11, 20, 23
    territory lost after World War I **4**, 5
Goering, Herman Wilhelm 34
Guernica 35, **35**
gold standard 20
Greece 48

Harding, Warren 9, **9**
Hitler, Adolf **25**, **26**, 27, 30, 31, 32, 34, 35, 36, 37,
    37, 38, 46, 48, 49, 51, 52
    Mein Kampf 28, 36
    Munich *Putsch* 23, 24
    rise to power 23, 24
Hull, Cordell 46, 54

Italy 7, 12–13, 31, 34, 51
    armed forces 31
    entry into World War II 41, 48
    foreign policy 13, 32

influence in Albania 13
involvement in Spanish Civil War 34
occupation of Abyssinia 32
occupation of Corfu 13

Japan 7, 9, 16–17, 18, 19, 21, 40–41, 50, 51
    alliances 17
    campaign in China 19, 42–3, 44, 45, 50
    foreign policy 16, 17, 40, 55
    invasion of French Indochina 51
    pact with Germany 43
    pact with Germany and Italy 50
    Pearl Harbor, attack on **50**, 51
    war with Soviet Union 16, **16**, **17**, 44–5
    warrior code 40

Kai-shek, Chiang **18**, 19, **19**, 40, 41, 44, 45, 50
Kellog, Frank 9
King George V 10
King George VI 37
Kuomintang (KMT) 19, 40, 41
Kwantung army 40, 41, 42

Laval, Pierre 32
League of Nations 6–7, 8, 32, 39, 41, 46, 52, 53, 55
    collective security 6, 30, 46
    Covenant 6, 32
    members of 7, 8, 16, 23, 28, 41
Lenin, Vladimir Ilyich 14, **14**, 15, 54, 55
Lloyd George, David 4, 10, **52**, 54
London Naval Treaty 40
Luftwaffe 34, 35

Maginot Line **30**, 31
Manchuria 17, 18, 19, 40, 41, 42
Mongolia 18, 44
Moscow 48, **48**
Munich Agreement **36**, 37
Mussolini, Benito 12–13, **13**, 31, 32, 34, 36, 52, 53, 54
    rise to power 12

Nazi Party 23, 24, 26–7, 28, **29**, 36, 54, 55
    membership of 27
    propaganda campaign 24, **24**
Netherlands 48
New Deal **21**
North Africa 48

Paris Peace Conference 4, 8, 10
Pearl Harbor **50**, 51

Poland 38, 39, 48

Reichstag 24, 26, **27**
Rhineland 11, 32, **33**
Rome-Berlin Axis 34
Roosevelt, Franklin D. 46, **47**, 51, 55
Ruhr 11, **11**, 22

SA 27
Soviet Union 4, 7, 14–15, 18, 19, 23, 34, 36, 38, 42, 43, 44, 45, 48, 51
    communist revolution 14
    invasion by Germany 38–9
    isolationism 15
    pact with Germany 38–9
    war with Japan 16, 17, 17
Spanish Civil War 34–5, 53
squadrisi 12
SS 27, **28**
Stalin, Joseph 15, 19, 38, **38**, 48, 49, **54**, 55
    rise to power 15
Stimson, Henry 46
Stresemann, Gustav 23, **23**, 28, 55
Sudetenland 36, 37

Tojo, Hideki **41**, 51, 55
Treaty of Locarno 23, 32
Treaty of Versailles 5, 8, 10, 22, 23, 28, 53, 54
trench warfare 10
Triple Entente 4
Trotsky, Leon 15, **15**, 55

United States 4, 7, 8–9, 16, 17, 20, 23, 41, 43, 46–7, 48, 49, 50, 51
    entry into World War II 51
    isolationism 8–9, 46–7
    Neutrality Acts 46
    rearmament 47
    war debts 9, 14
USS *Panay* 43

von Hindenburg, Field Marshal 26, 27
von Papen, Franz 25
von Ribbentrop, Joachim 38, **38**, 55
von Schuschnigg, Chancellor 36

Wall Street Crash 20, 24
World War I 4, 6, 10, 12, 14, 20, 30, 36, 55
    armistice 4